Sunnyvista City

Peter Viney

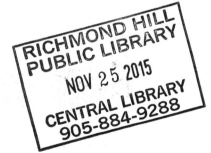

Garnet
Oracle

Garnet
EDUCATION

Peter Viney – author of this book, and Series Editor of the Garnet Oracle Readers – has over 40 years' experience teaching English and writing ELT materials. He now combines his writing with lecturing and teacher-training commitments internationally. He has authored and co-authored many successful textbook series and developed a wide range of highly popular video courses. Peter has been series editor and author on a number of graded reader series, and has also published with Garnet Education the highly popular *Fast Track to Reading*.

Published by
Garnet Publishing Ltd.
8 Southern Court
South Street
Reading RG1 4QS, UK

www.garneteducation.com

Copyright © Garnet Publishing Ltd 2014

ISBN 978 1 90757 524 2

British Cataloguing-in-Publication Data
A catalogue record for this book is available from the British Library.

Production

Series editor:	Peter Viney
Editorial:	Clare Chandler, Lucy Constable
Design and layout:	Mike Hinks
Illustration:	Rory O'Neil
Photography:	iStockphoto

Every effort has been made to trace copyright holders and we apologize in advance for any unintentional omission. We will be happy to insert the appropriate acknowledgements in any subsequent editions.

Printed and bound in Lebanon by International Press: interpress@int-press.com

1 Another perfect day

Suddenly he was awake.

He could see the light through the curtains. Tina was still sleeping beside him. That was strange. They always woke up together. He looked at his watch. Six thirty. He tried to think. Yes, they always woke up at exactly eight o'clock. He couldn't remember waking up before eight … not ever. But why not? Everybody in the city woke up at exactly eight o'clock every day.

He got out of bed quietly. Tina didn't move. He walked to the window and opened the curtains. He looked out at the quiet city. Nothing was moving. Then he went to the chair and sat down. He had to think. He had to remember. He was still sitting there an hour and a half later when Tina opened her eyes.

'Dan,' she said. 'Dan, what are you doing?'

'I got up early,' he said. Early. It sounded so strange. But why did it sound strange?

'Dan, is anything wrong?'

'Wrong? No, nothing's wrong. I just wanted to get up, that's all.'

Tina dressed. She smiled brightly. 'It's time for breakfast,' she said. 'Come on, we mustn't be late.'

'Wh...' He was going to say, 'Why not?' But he didn't. He stood up. 'Yes, it's time for breakfast. Look, you go down for breakfast. I'm not hungry. I'll see you later.'

Tina frowned. 'We have to go to breakfast. Are you feeling ill? I'll call the doctor.'

The doctor. He didn't want to see the doctor. So he had to go to breakfast. Tina was standing by the door. She looked annoyed.

'Tina,' he said, 'you don't understand. I didn't eat anything yesterday or the day before. And I feel different.'

Tina moved towards the phone. 'Of course you feel different, Dan. You *are* ill. I'll get the doctor right now.'

'Don't call, Tina ... please,' he said. 'I wanted to feel hungry. I haven't felt hungry for ... for a long time. I wanted to remember the feeling.'

She looked more annoyed. 'I really don't understand. No one wants to feel hungry.'

'That's it. Exactly! Nobody wants to feel hungry, nobody wants to feel unhappy, nobody wants to feel anything. Yesterday and the day before, I didn't eat. I haven't eaten for two days. Nobody noticed. I threw the food away ... and now I'm beginning to remember things. I think there's something in the food, a drug of some kind. Because of the drug we can't remember things.'

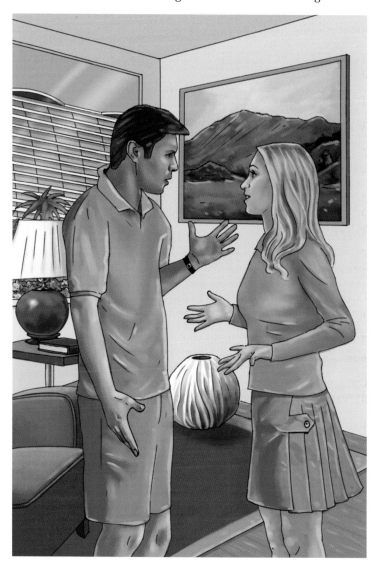

Tina's face was red. 'You're crazy,' she said quietly. 'That's impossible.'

'Maybe I *am* crazy,' he said, 'but why can't we remember things? What is this place?'

'It's ... it's our home,' she said slowly. 'All our friends are here.'

'Our home? Right. So when did we come here?'

'Oh, I don't know, Dan. A long time ago. Is it important?'

'Where were we before we came here?' He shook her arm angrily. 'Why did we come here?'

'Ow! Let go. You're hurting my arm,' she said.

'I'm sorry, but answer my question.'

'We came ... um, we ... Oh, Dan, I can't remember. Don't worry about it. Look, don't be silly. We're going to be very busy today. First there's our pottery class. You'll be able to finish making that bowl, and I can finish painting my plate. Then we're going swimming, then it'll be lunchtime. We can lie beside the swimming pool before tennis. Then there's dinner. Then we can play card games or dominoes and come to bed. It's going to be another perfect day. We'll be exhausted!'

'Exhausted? At eight o'clock in the evening?'

'Well, yes. That's bedtime. We need twelve hours sleep a night. Everybody knows that.'

'Tina, how long have we been here?'

'I don't know, Dan.'

'OK, we call this place "home". Don't you remember? We used to call it "a holiday". We used to call this "our hotel room". Now we call it "home".'

'I don't remember that.' She shook her head. 'No, that's stupid!'

'No, it isn't, Tina. I remembered that this morning, when I woke up early.'

Tina smiled. 'Ah, that explains everything! Perhaps you didn't wake up, Dan. Perhaps you had a strange dream, that's all.'

'But I did wake up, Tina. You saw me. I was sitting in that chair, with all my clothes on.'

She frowned. 'I'm not sure. Were you? I can't remember now.' Then she smiled. 'Come on! The sun's shining. It's another beautiful day. Let's go and have breakfast!'

She opened the door. Dan looked at her for a moment. 'You've forgotten our conversation, haven't you?' he said. 'You've forgotten it already.'

'Don't be silly,' she replied.

Dan went to the door too. 'Anyway, I'm really sorry for hurting your arm,' he said.

'My arm? Which arm? You didn't hurt my arm,' she said.

Dan could still see the red mark from his fingers.

2 I love cornflakes!

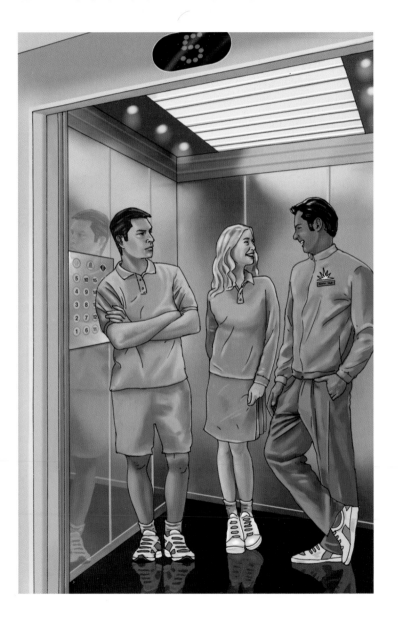

Dan followed her into the corridor. He looked at the line of doors on both sides. They were all exactly the same. They walked along to the lift. Tina pushed the button, and the doors opened.

'Morning, Tina, morning, Dan.' Russell, the sports organizer, was already in the lift. He smiled. 'I hope you're both ready for the tennis match,' he said. 'We're playing Level Fourteen this afternoon. They've got some good players.'

Tina laughed. 'Level Five ... Level Five,' she sang, 'Level Five is really alive!' It was their team song.

The lift went down to the restaurant on Level One. They joined the long line of people. They were all waiting for breakfast. Dan looked around. All the men were wearing shorts and T-shirts, and all the women were wearing skirts and tops. Dan looked down at his T-shirt. It was light blue, the Level Five colour. His shorts were light blue too. There were different colours for each level. The man in front of him was wearing a dark green Level Nine T-shirt. The woman behind him was wearing a light brown Level Sixteen top.

'Oh, good!' said Tina. 'Cornflakes! I love cornflakes.'

'So do I,' said Russell.

Dan smiled. Every day their breakfast was cornflakes with thin milk. Every day Tina seemed pleased and surprised with it. She always seemed pleased with lunch too. And dinner. Everybody seemed pleased at every mealtime. Dan thought about the food. Lunch was either tomato soup or potato soup, with some bread. Dinner was usually rice with some vegetables, or sometimes pasta with a little meat or fish. But they were never hungry.

Dan took a plastic tray, and put a bowl of cornflakes and a glass of orange juice on it. Well, they called it orange juice. It was sweet, orange-coloured water really. They had the same drink with every meal. He followed Tina and Russell towards the tables. The restaurant had big windows, and through them you could see the long swimming pool. The families with children all lived in the building on the other side of the pool. On this side there were only people without children. Dan stopped and thought, 'And none of us ever have children. And the youngest children on the other side are ten or eleven years old. They used to be younger. There used to be babies. Dan could remember babies. So no children are born here, and the youngest children are ten or eleven.' Dan waited for a moment. He put his tray down on an empty table. It was difficult. Thinking was so difficult. 'So maybe that's how long we've been here, ten or eleven years.'

He felt pleased with himself. He looked around quickly. Nobody was watching him. He picked up his tray again and walked over to the waste bin. Quickly he threw the food and drink away and put the empty tray down. He looked around again. No, nobody saw him. He started to walk towards Tina's table. 'And there are no sick people,' he thought. 'They take them to hospital. Nobody else leaves. Never.' He stopped. There was Jack! Jack went to hospital once ... but when? He walked over to Jack's table.

'Jack! Good morning!' he said.

'Good morning, Dan. Lovely day, isn't it?'

'How's your leg, Jack. Is it better?'

Jack looked surprised. 'My leg? There's nothing wrong with my leg.'

'Don't you remember, Jack? You hurt your leg. You had an accident by the swimming pool. You fell on a bottle and it broke, and it cut your leg badly. I was with you. There was blood everywhere. They took you to hospital. You went in a helicopter.'

Jack stopped eating. He looked worried for a moment. Then he laughed. 'I've never been to hospital in my life,' he said, 'and I've never been in a helicopter. Is this a joke?'

Dan looked down. Jack was wearing yellow Level Twelve shorts. He could see the long red mark on Jack's leg. He looked at Jack again. Jack was smiling.

'Dan ...' He looked round. Tina was standing behind him. 'Have you had your breakfast yet?' she asked.

'Yes,' he said carefully. 'I ate it with you just a moment ago. We had breakfast together. Don't you remember?'

'Oh, yes,' she said, 'of course. We had cornflakes. They were lovely!'

'Dan, are you all right?' Russell was there too. He was standing next to Tina.

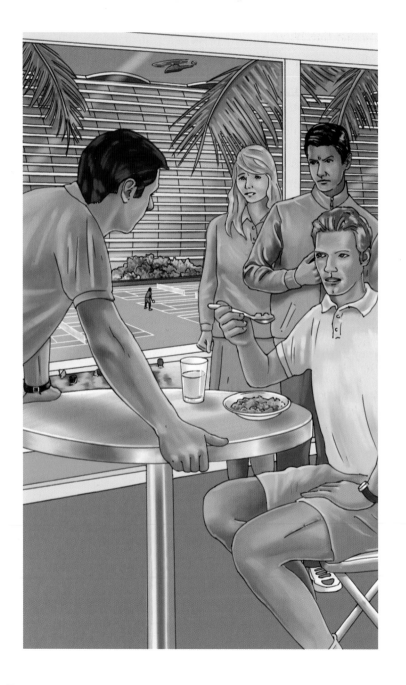

'Yes, I'm fine. Why?'

'I had breakfast with Tina just now. You weren't there.'

Dan thought hard. So Russell didn't forget things like all the others. That was interesting.

'I was just talking to Jack. About his leg. He cut his leg when we were at the swimming pool. Look, there's the red mark. You remember, Russell. He fell on a bottle. We carried him to the lift together. Then you went up to the roof. And a helicopter came.'

Russell wasn't smiling. 'Dan, could you come to my office after breakfast? I want to talk to you.'

Dan looked at Russell carefully. Russell was the sports organizer for Level Five. There were a lot of organizers. There were organizers for sport, pottery, music, yoga, everything. The organizers all lived on the highest level of the building, Level Twenty.

'No, sorry, I can't come to your office, Russell. I'm too busy.'

Russell looked surprised. 'Busy? What do you mean?'

Dan turned and walked quickly out of the restaurant. He got to the lifts and pushed the button. A lift door opened immediately. Dan stepped in. Russell was hurrying along the corridor towards him. Dan pushed a button and the doors closed. He looked at the line of buttons. He pushed number twenty.

3 Up on the roof

The buildings of Sunnyvista City were on both sides of a deep valley. The swimming pools, gardens and sports areas were at the bottom of the valley. The bedrooms were in the buildings on twenty levels. At both ends of the valley were office buildings. The city was about two kilometres long with many sections. Dan and Tina's room was in Section M. Each section had its own level teams, and people from different sections never met. Helicopters flew into the city every day. They always landed on the roof of the twentieth level. You could see them from the bottom of the valley.

The lift stopped. Dan walked out. It was his first visit to the twentieth level. The corridor was empty. The rooms were bigger here. There was a greater distance between the doors. Then he

heard a noise. It was a bell. The door of the next lift was opening. Dan stepped back. Russell came out.

'Dan,' said Russell. 'What are you doing here, my friend? This is Level Twenty. You shouldn't be here.'

'Why not?' said Dan. 'And why are you following me?'

'I have to speak to you,' said Russell, 'it's important.'

Russell's eyes were looking past Dan. He was looking at the wall next to the lift. There was a large red button on the wall. Russell was moving towards the button. Dan stepped between Russell and the button. 'OK,' said Dan, 'where shall we talk?'

Russell looked worried. 'Er … we can go to my office and talk there.'

Dan thought for a moment. Russell was bigger than Dan and stronger too. Dan thought about the sports in Sunnyvista City. Nobody tried to win, not ever. He could remember the day he played tennis against Russell. Dan tried to win. He wanted to win. Russell was surprised then. Dan smiled. 'Yes, come on. Let's go to your office. I mustn't be late for my pottery class. I'm making a bowl, a soup bowl. It's a lovely blue-green colour. Have you seen it?'

Russell smiled. 'No, I haven't. I'd like to see it. You can show me later.'

Dan stepped into the lift, and Russell followed him. Russell turned to the line of buttons next to the door. 'Level One,' he said to himself and moved his hand towards the button. Dan hit him once, hard on the back of the head, and Russell fell to the floor. His eyes were closed.

'I knocked him out,' thought Dan. 'I hit him once and knocked him out. Where did I learn that?'

There were never any fights in Sunnyvista City. Nobody was ever angry. Dan looked at the buttons. He pushed the button for Level Ten. There was nobody on Level Ten at this time of the morning. He stepped quickly out of the lift. The lift was going to go to Level Ten.

Dan ran along the corridor. He heard the lift doors. They were closing. There were some stairs at the end. He ran up the stairs. There was a door at the top. He pushed the door and it opened. It wasn't locked! He went through the door and he was on the roof.

A large helicopter was standing on the roof. Dan stopped and looked at it. He recognized it immediately. It was a Westing Type 23. He tried to remember. Yes, the Westing Type 23 could carry twenty-eight passengers, it had two engines and could fly at 300 kilometres an hour. It was fast for a helicopter. But how did he know all that? He tried hard to think. Of course! He used to work at a helicopter factory. He used to make Westing helicopters. He worked on the Type 23. He used to work? But when was that? And where? Why did he stop working? Why did he come to Sunnyvista City?

And there was another problem. The Westing Type 23 was the newest, most modern helicopter from his factory. But this one looked quite old. It needed new paint. There were dirty black marks around the engines. Ten or eleven years old? Probably.

Dan walked across the roof. It was very wide. He walked to the side and looked over the wall and down at Sunnyvista City. Then he walked across the roof and looked over the opposite side. He shook his head. There was another valley with more buildings. It

looked exactly like Sunnyvista City. There was a door on that side too, with a notice on it, 'Sortie'. He tried to think. He knew it meant 'exit'. The door he came out of had a sign with 'Exit' on it. 'Sortie' was French. But when did he learn French? He ran over to the helicopter. The door was open. He climbed the steps. There were a lot of boxes inside. Dan climbed in and hid behind the boxes. There was writing on the boxes. The nearest ones to the door said 'Sunnyvista City'. Others said 'Club de Soleil'. Then others said 'Playa del Sol'. He thought about the writing. English, French and Spanish. Strange. Then he looked at some more boxes. Some were German, some were Italian and some were Portuguese.

The door to the front of the helicopter was open. Dan could see through to the controls and the pilots' seats. There were several computer screens. He remembered. Everything was automatic. The Westing Type 23 could almost fly itself. Screens. Yes! There were no television screens or computer screens in Sunnyvista City. There were no films, no computer games. That's why they played cards or old games after dinner, like dominoes or snakes and ladders. No films. Films bring back memories of other places and other times. You can see all the things that aren't in Sunnyvista City, like streets and cars and fields and normal houses. Computer games are often about fighting or winning a game. Yes, screens show you all the things that aren't in Sunnyvista City. Things like love and hate.

Dan sat very still for about ten minutes then he heard voices. The door closed. Two men were in the front of the helicopter.

'Well, that's it. We've taken everything to the English and French cities.'

'Great. We'll do the German and Spanish cities tomorrow.'

4 Should I stay or should I go?

The engines started and he couldn't hear anything else. The helicopter took off and climbed slowly into the sky. Dan moved quietly to the window and looked out. The sky was blue. The sun was shining and there were no clouds. He could see more valleys like Sunnyvista City, then more and more. There were no roads into the valleys. That was strange. They flew over the valleys for half an hour. Then Dan could see roads and trees and fields and farms. In the far distance he could see a town with factories and smoke.

The helicopter began to go down. Dan hid behind the boxes again. The helicopter landed and the door opened. Three men climbed in and began to move the boxes. Dan stood up. 'Hello,' he said. 'Where are we?'

The men looked at each other. They didn't speak. A woman climbed into the helicopter. 'It's OK,' she said to the men, 'it's another one from the valleys.' She turned to Dan. 'Why have you come here?'

'I'm not sure. I started to remember things. I wanted to remember more,' said Dan.

'You've come from Sunnyvista City, haven't you?' said the woman.

Dan nodded his head.

'Hmm. I think you should come with me.'

Dan followed the woman out of the helicopter.

'My name's Travis, Jenny Travis,' said the woman. 'Come on, we'll go to my office.'

Dan looked around. They were at a small airport. He could see nine or ten helicopters, two large jet planes and a lot of trucks. The helicopters were all Westing Type 23s. People were putting

boxes into them. There were mountains around the airport and a small road going towards the town in the distance.

Jenny Travis took Dan to a small building. It was old and dirty outside. She led him into a small untidy office. There were books and old newspapers and magazines everywhere. Dan was surprised. In Sunnyvista City everything was always in the right place. Everything was clean and tidy. Nothing was ever dirty or untidy. There were only a few books and there was only one newspaper. It appeared every day. It had just one page, and was called *What's On in Sunnyvista City*. The news in it was the same every day, just a list of who played in the sports matches.

'Sit down,' she said. 'Would you like something to drink? I've got tea or coffee. And maybe I can find some egg sandwiches in the fridge.'

'Er, no, thank you,' said Dan.

She laughed. 'Don't worry. There's nothing in the food or drink. I'm sure you're very hungry and very thirsty.'

'How do you know that?' asked Dan.

Jenny Travis sat down behind her desk. Dan noticed she looked exhausted, her clothes were old, her hair was untidy and some of it was grey. Nobody looked tired in Sunnyvista City, and they all went to the hairdresser once a week.

'People like you are always hungry and thirsty,' she said, 'that's why they're here. Look, don't worry. Sunnyvista City isn't a prison, you know. When the helicopter took off, the pilots knew there was somebody on board immediately. The helicopter was heavier.'

'Why didn't they take me back?'

'I've told you. It isn't a prison. You got into the helicopter because you wanted to leave. That's OK. You've left. We didn't stop you.'

Dan looked at the desk for a moment. 'There was a man, one of the sports organizers. His name's Russell. He tried to stop me. I knocked him out, and I left him in the lift and then I sent the lift down to Level Ten. I didn't want to hurt him.'

'He's OK. He isn't happy. He's got a headache, but you didn't hurt him badly. I spoke to him on the phone a few minutes ago.'

'What is Sunnyvista City?' asked Dan. 'What is it really?'

'How much can you remember?' she said.

'I'm beginning to remember more and more. I can't remember everything yet.'

'You'll remember more tomorrow,' said Jenny Travis. 'Let me get you a coffee and a sandwich.'

Dan sat still while she made the coffee, and got a sandwich from the fridge. He looked at the sandwich, but didn't touch it. She broke a piece off and ate it. 'See ... there's nothing wrong with it.' Then she drank a little from his coffee cup. 'Now do you believe me?'

Dan ate the sandwich hungrily and drank some coffee. 'I'm beginning to remember more,' he said.

'Tell me.'

'Well,' started Dan. 'I used to work in a helicopter factory, the Westing factory in my home town ... but this is a different country, isn't it?'

'Yes, it's a different country,' she replied. 'Go on.'

'I lost my job,' said Dan. 'The factory had new automatic systems. They didn't need many workers. I was unemployed for a long time. Then I saw an advertisement on television. It was for very cheap thirty-day holidays in the sun for the unemployed. We flew to Sunnyvista City. It was a long flight, then we took a helicopter to the city and we started our holiday. I can't remember much after that. But I remember something. I haven't seen or talked about money for years. Not since we arrived there.'

She nodded. 'Sunnyvista is one of the oldest cities here. It opened ten years ago. You haven't seen money for ten years.'

'But what's happening?' said Dan.

'Can you remember ten or fifteen years ago? Think back. There were millions of unemployed people in the world. Very few people had jobs, because there was little work. Computers did everything. There was fighting in the streets. There were wars. Many, many people died. People were bored and hungry and angry everywhere. The governments all over the world had a meeting, a secret meeting. They built Sunnyvista City and hundreds of places like it. All of them were in warm, sunny places. Many people worked to build the cities, so there were fewer unemployed people. Then they sent the unemployed people on "holidays". They gave everyone drugs in their food. There were no hungry people, no fighting and no children in the cities. There was also no memory. Nobody could remember anything. Everybody lived for today.'

'That's terrible!' said Dan.

'Is it? Is it really?' she said. 'Things were much worse before.'

'Are you going to send me back?' asked Dan.

'You can choose. We can give you a drug. You'll wake up tomorrow in your room in Sunnyvista City, and you won't remember me, or anything about this place or this conversation.'

'You said I can choose,' said Dan.

'Yes, you can stay here. You can go back to your hometown, if you like. We'll find you a job. You know a lot about helicopters. Maybe you can work here. Life will be difficult. You'll have to work hard. There'll be no more lying by the swimming pool, or swimming or tennis.'

'But I'll be free,' said Dan.

'Yes, you will. A few people … only one or two per cent … leave Sunnyvista City and the other cities every year. That isn't a problem. We can find jobs for those people. But most people are happy in the holiday cities. More than half the people who leave choose to go back.'

'I don't believe it,' said Dan.

'You will. Maybe next year you'll want to go back. It's an easy life. We can find you a job as an organizer in the cities, if you like. We need lots of them.'

'I was thinking about the organizers. They know what Sunnyvista City is, right?'

'Of course.'

'They eat the same food. They eat with us. How does that happen?'

'Think,' she said. 'Did they ever drink the orange juice? Or the water in your rooms?'

'No … Russell hated orange juice … oh, I understand. I couldn't do his job. That's the worst thing. He's lying to people all day every day.'

'I know,' she said. 'I was an organizer for two years. Not at Sunnyvista City, actually. I worked at Happy Valley. It's not far away. I couldn't do that job either. I hated it. But what about now? Are you going back or are you staying here?'

Dan sat back in his seat and smiled. 'I'll stay here,' he said.

Glossary

These extra words are not in the 1,000 words for Level 3.

annoyed a little bit angry

conversation a talk between two or more people

cornflakes a special breakfast food; *Kelloggs Cornflakes* is the most famous make

corridor a long narrow space inside a building with doors on both sides

curtains large pieces of cloth over the windows of a room – you can close them at night

distance the space between two places or things

dominoes a game with small pieces of wood with dots on for numbers

drug 1) a medicine or chemical from a pharmacy that can make sick people well, or 2) a dangerous thing that people take, which is against the law; in this story it is a special drug that makes people forget

easy the opposite of difficult

exhausted very, very tired

factory a building where people make things, usually with machines

government the organization that controls a country

hairdresser a person who cuts hair

helicopter a machine that flies, and which can move straight up or straight down

knock (someone) out hit someone so that they are asleep with their eyes closed

level a floor of a large building, or of a car park

mark something you can see: *A pen makes a mark on paper; After you cut your leg, there will be a mark because of the cut*

match a game, we usually say *tennis match* not *tennis game*

organizer someone who plans or controls things for other people

pottery making things like cups, plates, bowls, etc., using clay

section part of something

shorts short trousers

snakes and ladders a game where you have to go down snakes and go up ladders

soup a food made with water that you eat with a spoon

swimming pool a special place where you can swim

tidy everything in the correct place

tray a flat piece of plastic, metal or wood for carrying plates, cups, glasses, etc.

unemployed without a job

untidy the opposite of tidy

waste bin something you can put rubbish (or trash) in

Activities

1 **Look at the story again and find this information. How fast can you find it?**

   1 The time people wake up in Sunnyvista City.

   2 The time people go to bed in Sunnyvista City.

   3 The age of the youngest children in Sunnyvista City.

   4 How long Sunnyvista City is from one end to the other.

   5 The colour of Level Five clothes.

   6 The number of passengers the helicopter can carry.

   7 The top speed of the helicopter.

   8 The French word for 'exit'.

   9 The number of days in the holiday which Dan saw an advertisement for.

   10 The number of people that leave Sunnyvista City (per cent).

2 **Are these sentences true (✓) or false (✗)? Correct the false ones.**

   1 ☐ The special drug was in the food.

   2 ☐ No children are born in Sunnyvista City.

   3 ☐ Jack has never been to hospital.

   4 ☐ Tina could remember coming to the city.

   5 ☐ Russell knew why they were there.

   6 ☐ The organizers lived on Level Ten.

7 ☐ Russell was badly hurt in an accident.

8 ☐ The pilots didn't know that Dan was in the helicopter.

9 ☐ Jenny Travis used to work in Sunnyvista City.

10 ☐ Dan will go back to Sunnyvista City next year.

3 Complete the sentences with words from the glossary.

1 Breakfast was always _____ with thin milk.

2 When he woke up, Dan could see light through the _____.

3 Dan was wearing a light blue T-shirt and _____.

4 Lunch was usually tomato or potato _____.

5 Dan was making a bowl in the _____ class.

6 Dan used to work in a helicopter _____.

7 There was a red _____ on Jack's leg from the accident.

8 There were twenty _____ in Dan and Tina's building.

9 Millions of people lost their jobs. They were _____.

10 Jenny Travis's office wasn't tidy. It was very _____.

4 Do these comprehension tasks.

1 How long did Dan wait before Tina woke up?

2 Why didn't Dan want breakfast?

3 What did Dan do with his food the day before?

4 What is Russell's job?

5 What did people wear in Sunnyvista City?

6 How long did Dan live in Sunnyvista City?

7 What happened to Jack by the swimming pool?

8 Who carried Jack to the lift?

9 Where did the organizers live?

10 Why was Russell following Dan?

11 Why did Russell move towards the red button on the wall?

12 How did Dan knock Russell out?

13 What did Dan use to do before he came to Sunnyvista City?

14 Where did Dan hide in the helicopter?

15 How did the pilots know that Dan was there?

16 Where did Jenny Travis take Dan?

17 Why did Dan go to Sunnyvista City?

18 Why did the governments build Sunnyvista City?

19 What was the world like before they built the cities?

20 What is Dan going to do?

5 Discuss these questions.

1 Describe a normal day in Sunnyvista City.

2 Describe the city.

3 Describe the meals. What were they like?

4 Describe how Dan left Sunnyvista City.

5 Describe the world ten years before the story.

6 Was Sunnyvista City a good idea or a bad idea? Why?

6 Imagine ...

What about Tina? What is she going to do? Is Dan going to leave her in Sunnyvista City or not?

_____

_____

_____

_____

_____

_____

_____

_____

_____

_____

_____

_____

_____

_____

_____

_____

_____

Other titles available in the series

Garnet Oracle — Level 1

The Collector

The Locked Room

The Watchers

Zoo Diary

Garnet Oracle — Level 2

Casualty!

Strawberry and The Sensations

Underground

The Visit

Garnet Oracle — Level 3

African Adventure

Life Lines

Milo

Sunnyvista City

Garnet Oracle — Level 4

The Case of the Dead Batsman

The Hitchhiker

Space Romance

A Tidy Ghost